Distance

Nathanael O'Reilly

Distance

PICARO PRESS

Acknowledgements

Special thanks to Sean Scarisbrick, Tricia Jenkins, and Alex Lemon for reading and critiquing earlier versions of this book – especially Alex, who brought his amazing energy and unique perspective to the revision process. Thanks to Jonathan Bennett, Paul Kane and Lachlan Brown for sharing readings in Toronto and Portland; it was a pleasure and an honour.

Many of the poems in this collection previously appeared in the following publications (sometimes in a different form): *Australian Love Poems, Blackmail Press, The Blue Fog Poetry Journal, Cordite Poetry Review, The Disappearing, LiNQ, Meanderings, Page Seventeen, PRISM, Prosopisia, Red River Review, Snorkel, Social Alternatives, Southern Ocean Review, Taj Mahal Review, Tincture, Transnational Literature*, and *Windmills*. Many thanks to the editors of these publications, and especially to Rob Riel and Picaro Press.

Distance
ISBN 978 1 74027 997 0
Copyright © text Nathanael O'Reilly 2015

First published by Picaro Press 2014

This edition published 2015 by
Picaro Press – an imprint of
GINNINDERRA PRESS
PO Box 3461 Port Adelaide 5015 Australia
www.ginninderrapress.com.au

Contents

Australia	9
Crabbing	11
Doncaster, 1977	13
Ballarat Scenes	14
Floodwaters	18
Moreton Bay	19
Suburban Fantasy	20
First Kill	21
Saturday Night on the Goulburn	23
Falling Through Uncertainty	24
Near Drowning	26
Closer	27
Fruit Picking	28
Cider Buzz	30
French Accent	31
Sinking	32
Tzatziki	33
Secular Baptism	34
The Pastor and His Daughter	35
The Keating Years	37
Concert-going	38
Flinders Street Scene	39
Rosehill	41
Lost Suitcase	42
Your Funeral	43
Europe	47
Transitory	49
Ayr	50
Blank Faces	51

Slaving	52
Islington Dawn	53
Pozières	54
North Rhine-Westphalia	55
The Hill of Tara	57
Invisible Borders	58
St John's Wood	60
Skimming	62
York	63
Yorkshire Lunch	64
Côte d'Azur	65
America	**67**
At the Hair Salon in Big Sandy, Texas	69
Blue	70
Disintegration	71
The Woods	72
House Sitting	73
Michigan	77
Reminders	79
Cupcakes and Monsters	80
Free	81
Rosemary and Gasoline	82
Cancer in Suburbia	83
Christian Girls	84
West Texas	85
Hybridity	86
Reunions	87
Expat Christmas	88

For Tricia & Celeste,

Mum & Dad,

Sean,

and the good friends who have shared my journey

Australia

Crabbing

For Greg Conlon 1974–2004

Sitting on the docks
by the Moyne, we knot
fishing line round chunks
of beef, lower them
down through the water
between the rocks
beside the pylons,
tempting crabs.

Fishing boats moored
nearby rock gently.
We try to pronounce
Russian and Norwegian names,
baffled by the distance
the boats have travelled –
from the top to the bottom
of the earth just to fish.

On the northern shore
of the Southern Ocean
we look towards Antarctica,
unable to grasp
the vastness of space,
where fishermen trawl
far above their prey.

Tugging on our lines,
the crabs surrender.
We draw them up
into the air,
deposit them into buckets,
impressed by our ability
to take them out of their world.

Doncaster, 1977

When I lived next door to Max Walker
I went to the Royal Melbourne Show,
came home with a cowboy hat
made of pink cardboard. After playing
Cowboys and Indians in the backyard
I hung my hat high in a tree –
the overnight rain transformed
substance. In the morning I shimmied
up the trunk and out onto the branch
to retrieve my prized possession,
slipped from the wet black bough
and fell headfirst onto the concrete
patio. Mum was in the shower
enjoying solitude when my brother
burst into the bathroom screaming
He's covered in blood! He broke his head!
Rushing out the door to the hospital,
kids walking up our driveway clutching
miniature souvenir cricket bats called
– Is this where Max lives?

Ballarat Scenes

I

Lying awake in a shared bedroom
on the corner of Waller
and Pleasant watching
beams of light arc across the wall.

II

Burning tongues sipping
tomato soup at recess
shivering in the shelter shed
at Redan Primary School.

III

Breaking Ian's thumb
attempting to take a mark
during kick-to-kick on the oval
at lunchtime during Grade One.

IV

Riding the bus with mum
to Wendouree Village, scarfing
crinkle-cut hot chips, posing for photos
in a replica of the Red Baron's biplane.

V

Going to school on International
Day dressed as an Arab
in a curtain Mum altered
on her sewing machine.

VI

Getting nipped on the bum
by a German shepherd climbing
the neighbour's grey picket fence
after retrieving a cricket ball.

VII

School excursions to Sovereign Hill,
the Eureka Stockade
and the fire station,
aiming hoses at passing cars.

VIII

Walking to Sebas Tech after school
to wait for Dad to finish work,
drive us home past soccer
fields and the greyhound track.

IX

Listening to the seven-inch
of 'Up There Cazaly'
after school on a winter afternoon
in nineteen seventy-nine.

X

Climbing a gum tree near Grant's
parents' flat, carving our names
with pocketknives into a bough
with a view over Lake Wendouree.

XI

Buying croissants from the Vietnamese girl
who stood on a stool to reach the register
at the French bakery on the corner
at the bottom of Sturt near the bus stop.

XII

Shuffling home on a Friday night along
Lyons Street through piles of autumn
leaves carrying a bottle of Brown Brothers
Cabernet Sauvignon in a brown paper bag.

XIII

Dancing drunkenly in front of the fireplace
in a bedroom with two dozen friends
as the floor bounced and books and CDs
fell from the brick-and-plank shelves.

XIV

Walking through the cemetery towards
The Miller's Arms on winter evenings
looking for my surname on headstones
erected a century before my birth.

Floodwaters

Driving slowly through floodwaters
in northern New South Wales
in a 1979 Honda Civic hatchback,
watching the water spray against
the windows from the backseat,
too young to worry
about the engine stalling,
driving off the bitumen,
or the depth of the water.
Creeping forward, waves
spread from our car
through the endless darkness
over the submerged plain.
The headlights reflected
off the rippling water
and the Southern Cross shone
high above the highway.

Moreton Bay

Four boys and two fathers,
we set up our rods and tackle
on the fishing platform
near the end of the pier
at Redcliffe. Baiting my hook,
I stepped backwards
to avoid a mate's cast,
tripped over a rod and fell
into the depths, righting myself
as I sank, watching the light
above fade while I descended.
Suddenly
a hairy fist gripped my wrist,
dragging me towards life.
Another hand grasped my belt,
hoisting me through the surface
out into the air where my father's
hands grasped my armpits
and pulled me to his chest
where he knelt on the planks
surrounded by open-mouthed boys.

Suburban Fantasy

As pre-pubescent boys roaming
the suburbs on BMXs, searching
for excitement on long, hot Sundays,
we were simultaneously disgusted
and thrilled to discover used condoms
(Frenchies, rubbers, dingers)
on the dirt slope beneath
the squash courts behind the Underwood
Road shopping centre. The discarded
rubbers hinted at the sordid world of furtive
teenage sex going on all around us, yet
out of sight and out of our childish reach.
We perved on horny teens French-kissing
and groping underwater in public pools,
memorized tongue and finger techniques,
foolishly imagined we had a chance
with nubile bikini-clad classmates.

First Kill

Pressing the butt of the four-ten
into my shoulder I squint down the barrel,
sighting rabbits grazing beside the creek.
Convincing myself they're vermin,
ignoring innocence, I pick my target.

As I squeeze the trigger
the rabbit's guts burst open
splattering the Grassmere paddock
with blood, shit and entrails.

Blood surging, I race to my victim,
stand above its shallow breathing.
Trembling, I bring my Blundstone
down with full force, crunching
life from the soft white head.

Golden Fleece

Regaining consciousness
on the grimy floor inside

a Golden Fleece petrol station
outside West Wyalong

I observe other customers
observing me, all of us

wondering why I am
no longer standing in line

waiting to buy the Lifesavers
and the can of Fanta

that have escaped my hands
and rolled towards the door.

Saturday Night on the Goulburn

We camped on a sandbank
at a bend in the Goulburn
with a dozen classmates,
most of them not really mates,
just friends of friends.

We cooled our beer in the shallows
and sat round the bonfire
singing along to the ghetto-blaster
playing 'Midnight Blue'.

As the hours passed
piles of empty bottles multiplied,
couples drifted off to tents
or into the bush with blankets.

I sat in the cold sand
by the fire with the unattached,
wondering how to approach
the girl six feet away
who served as the subject
of my fantasies ever since
she touched my forearm
six months before and declared
she liked my T-shirt.

Unable to figure out
how to get started,
I sipped Southern Comfort
while she softly sang
'Never Tear Us Apart'.

Falling Through Uncertainty

After nightfall we pedalled
along country roads
to the Broken River,
dumped our bikes in the bush
near the giant rivergum
with the rope swing

One by one we gripped
the knot above our heads,
kept our fears to ourselves,
launched into the darkness
from the top of the bank
thirty feet above the river

We dropped down, out and away,
swinging
towards safety,
rushing over the snags
toward the deep,
our feet tucked up,
rose rapidly to the apex,
waiting for the right moment,
to release
the rope
and drop
down
towards
the water

not knowing
when
we would make

contact

Near Drowning

Half an hour into an afternoon
walk exploring the rock pools,
flotsam and caves
east of Logan's Beach

we rounded another headland
and found our party
of three one short.
My grandfather was gone.

We froze for a moment,
overpowered by the Southern Ocean.
Running back the way we came,
we rounded the headland again,

scanning the foot of the cliffs
and the roiling Antarctic water,
failing to discover
my father's father. Our shouts

echoed faintly from beyond
the rock shelf. Running
to the edge, I peered
over and down to find Pa

drenched, shaking, clinging
to the jagged rocks, trying
to clamber to safety before
the crash of another breaker.

I reached out, clasped his hand
in one of mine, gripped the rocks
behind with the other, hauled
my ancestor up onto his land.

Closer

The rains came and flushed
us from our tent in the field.
We sought refuge from the storm

in the car, where we lit candles
and read to each other from
an old collection of Yeats –

a gift from my grandfather.
As the rain drummed its tattoo
on the bonnet and the roof

we shared dreams and passions.
Long after midnight we climbed
into the backseat where we lay

together for the first time,
finally drifting off to sleep
as the storm began to clear.

Fruit Picking

During the summer holidays
I rose before dawn, helped
my father and brother load
the Commodore with drinks,
hats, sunscreen and sandwiches.
We drove towards Tatura,
Ardmona or Mooroopna,
orchards of apricots and pears.

Towed by the tractor, we rode
in empty bins to our row,
dismounted and shouldered ten-foot
ladders to the day's first tree.
Planting steel ladders beneath
branches heavy with fruit,
we climbed up to begin.

My canvas bag strained,
hung down to sweaty knees.
Leather straps cut into shoulders
as I waddled to the bin.

Each pear I picked,
each minute I balanced
on the ladder, my wants
grew closer. The stereo's price
dropped like a countdown.
The CD purchased song by song.
Skateboard parts acquired one by one.
The perfectly folded Levis
travelled towards my closet.

A thin layer of insecticide
coated the skins of the fruit,
blended with sweat and sunscreen
on our arms, making us ghosts.

At eleven we broke for lunch,
sitting cross-legged in the shade
amidst the stench of rotting fruit,
then jumped into the channel,
washing away chemicals and sweat
before returning to work.

Knocking off for the day at three,
we gave the foreman our tally
and went home to sleep through
the hottest hours of the afternoon.

At dinner, my brother and I shared
cold longnecks with Dad like men
who have earnt their rest
before retiring shirtless to the couch
for a lazy evening watching cricket.

Cider Buzz

for Chris

We met at the Cricketer's Arms
to work on a buzz before the Cure
concert with some girls from Deakin
Hall. Half an hour before the show
we bought two more Strongbows
each, stuffed them into our pockets
and set out across the fields towards
the MCG. Halfway to the Tennis
Centre we whacked the tops off
on a railing fence, wrapped
our lips around spurting bottles.
We knocked back our last ciders
beside the tennis courts,
carried our buzz inside
through the turnstiles to our seats.

French Accent

Coming home from the milk bar
with a Big M and *The Age,*
a girl sits smoking on the front steps,
knees drawn up to her chest.
She's here about the spare room.
I invite her inside, where she speaks
with a slight French accent, quoting
Rimbaud, Mallarmé and Baudelaire.
Over black coffee, she tells tales
of life as a diplomat's daughter
in Vanuatu and New Caledonia,
sits with her back to the window,
the afternoon sun in my eyes,
her face blackened by shadow.

Sinking

Lying on the floor
of a friend's room
in Whitley College
before dawn listening
to The Cure's 'Sinking'
after drinking and talking
all night about sex and religion
I feel my body disintegrating
oozing through the carpet
down through the concrete
dropping pleasantly
into the room below
as I meander in and out
of consciousness
knowing I have nowhere
I have to go and nothing
I have to be after sunrise

Tzatziki

In a Lebanese restaurant on Sydney Road
the pastor's daughter reaches under the table
and gives a hand job to the teenage boy
beside her. While her parents, two families
and a group of friends converse, break bread,
chew lamb, lick tzatziki sauce from fingers,
she nonchalantly moves her hand
under the tablecloth, talking and laughing.
Minutes later, the stunned recipient of her attentions
pushes his chair out, turns his back, scurries away.

Secular Baptism

The pastor's son spent
a winter weekend secluded
in his room wearing
inside-out pyjamas
with his new girlfriend
listening to Nick Cave
on repeat, emerging
only for shits and showers.
Lying beneath images
of Nirvana and The Cure
he tried on new versions
of himself in a dark room
soupy with incense and sweat.
The pastor's son attempted
to reject class conditioning
with forty-eight cans of VB,
Jim Beam and condoms
purchased with parents' money.
Southern gothic, religion,
rage, violence, sex, beauty
and the sublime combined
in the cauldron of seclusion –
a potent brew, but not strong enough
to cleanse twenty years of conformity.

The Pastor and His Daughter

The pastor drives you home
after the evening service
oblivious to your hand
inside his daughter's blouse
as she sits on your knee
behind him in the crowded
car. He does not feel her
heart rate accelerating
as your hand slides upward
through beads of sweat.
He does not hear her soft
urgent breath, nor is he aware
when her nipples harden
beneath the gentle caress
of reputedly harmless fingers,
the same fingers that gently
turned the pages of a pocket
edition of *Les Fleurs du Mal*
nestled inside the *Song of Solomon*
during his abstinence sermon.

The Backyard, the Coffee

While taking the rubbish out
beneath the bleak autumn sky
I decided to change my life
I hung my fears and doubts
beside the socks and jocks
and my favourite corduroy jeans
on the rusty clothesline
I watched them go limp and blue
as the leaves fell from the trees
and rolled across the backyard

I went inside for a coffee
defrosting my hands over the kettle
as it boiled and shook and steamed
like I did when she left me
and while the coffee brewed
I considered how we become ready
how we are consumed
by life and love and death
and sex and money and religion

But then the coffee was ready –
I drank it slowly, savouring
and all I could think about
was just how damn good she tasted
when I kissed her hungrily
on that midsummer night

The Keating Years

Autumn afternoons browsing in op shops
followed by cappuccinos and coffee scrolls
were the only luxuries we could afford
scraping by on Austudy in a 'regional city'

during the Keating years. We lived
in damp ninety-year-old weatherboard
houses shared with uni friends,
ate pasta, porridge and potatoes,

drank five-dollar port and cask wine.
We walked almost everywhere,
took the bus to campus; our parents
were the only people we knew with jobs.

Splurging meant spending ten bucks
on pots of VB, trying our luck
at a club after midnight
and sharing a taxi with mates.

Poverty taught us not to hope
for a better future. We knew the recession
we had to have meant our degrees qualified
us for nothing but the back of the dole queue.

Concert-going

We took Cortinas and Falcons
on whirlwind weekend road trips
up the Hume to catch concerts
in Sydney, stopping only
for petrol, sleeping entwined
on friends of friends' floors.

Beer-drenched Blundstones
crushed cans of Toohey's
beneath us as we gripped
the stage and braced our legs,
pushing against the punters
surging behind us, embracing
the girls cocooned in the space
our bodies created together.

Our concert T-shirts christened
with communal sweat, smoke and beer,
we revelled in the music's power,
got off on bass passing through
our bodies and the feedback
in our ears as we walked away,
arms around each other's shoulders.

Flinders Street Scene

The drunk stumbling
under the iconic clocks
at Flinders Street station
yells *Fuck you cunt!*
into the summer heat,
lurching towards teens
communing in the shade,
then back to the steps
where I stand alone.

Shaking a fist in my face,
he exclaims *You're*
the bastard! Ya cunt.
I'm gunna get ya!

Bystanders glance, avoid
catching the drunk's eye.
I am taller, stone
sober, so I stand
my ground, waiting
for a fist to swing,
the flash of a blade.

The clocks above silent
as the seconds pass.

The drunk turns and vomits
on the steps, splattering
a passenger's Myer bags.
I cross the street, enter
Young & Jackson's, order
a pot of Carlton Draught,
raise it to my lips
with trembling hand.

Rosehill

for Grant

We settled into the soft leather
of your factory fresh Alfa Romeo
and headed west on Parramatta Road,
bound for Rosehill. Once through
the turnstiles and inside the stands,
we examined the form guide, made
guesses, placed twenty dollar bets.
We staked a claim at a table outside
in the mid-winter sun, rolled sleeves
and tucked into meat pies and VB.
When the racing began, we migrated
to the edge of the track, leaning farther
over the rails as the horses rounded the bend
and charged down the home straight.
We shouted, jumped, pumped fists.
The ground shook, turf and sweat flew,
and the heaving mob charged past,
making us losers as they crossed the line.

Lost Suitcase

Home after two and a half years
overseas, I searched a garage
in Doncaster for a suitcase
with a turquoise tartan pattern,
the keeping place for hundreds
of letters received over a decade.
Bundles of letters contained
detailed histories of relationships,
exploits, fantasies, disappointments.
The news came from Tasmania,
Queensland, New South Wales,
Western Australia and Victoria.
Correspondents shared fractions
of their lives, quoted song lyrics,
poetry and scriptures, confessed
infatuations, revealed secrets.
I found the suitcase on a shelf
and opened the dusty lid, discovering
a continent emptied of friendships.

Your Funeral

for Dorothy Lola Quigley (1924–2010)

On the morning of your funeral
I rose at four-thirty from a hotel bed
in Sydney, dressed quickly and caught
the five o'clock train to the airport.
In Melbourne, I ran to catch the Skybus
into Southern Cross, then hustled
to the corner of Spencer and Collins
where my brother's car waited.

We drove the four hours to Port Fairy
without stopping, the landscape
as familiar as your kiss
after almost four decades
of journeys to your home.

We discussed how lucky we were
to see you three days before
you died, how we kissed you
on your forehead, whispered
I love you, Nana, and knew
we would never see you alive again.

We took the scenic route into town
past the golf links where you played,
then stopped at the East Beach
to check the surf. Unable to face
a house full of mourning relatives,
we changed into funeral clothes
in the healing air of the beach car park
like kids changing after a refreshing surf.

At St Patrick's, we walked the aisle
to our pew in the third row, shaking
hands, hugging and exchanging nods.
You lay in a closed coffin ten feet away,
where your husband lay less than four
years ago, inches from where my parents
were married. The priest swung incense
and delivered the requisite words
in a booming Dutch-Australian accent.

I wondered if you were wearing
your best Fletcher Jones outfit, forever loyal
to the man who measured your father
as he stood on his farmhouse kitchen table
and tailored a beautiful suit from the wool
shorn from your father's Merinos.

Your daughters, granddaughters,
and son-in-law all eulogized.
I read Tennyson's 'Crossing the Bar'.
Chris and I draped your coffin.

After you were carried to the hearse,
we gathered outside in the winter sun,
chatted sombrely with relatives,
neighbours and your patients,
roughly halfway between the cemetery
and the house you called home
for more than half a century.

We walked behind the hearse
to the grave site and congregated
around your grave as the priest
uttered his final words and you
were lowered slowly into the earth
beside your husband. One by one,
we dropped dirt and flowers
onto your coffin. The ritual
provided comfort, displacing grief.

I drank beer with uncles and cousins
at the wake in a bluestone building.
After years apart, we made small talk
about houses, holidays, sport and work.
As the sun went down over the Moyne
I realised that now you are gone
I am running out of reasons to return
to the place where I felt most at home.

Europe

Transitory

From below my window, in the square
where a statue of Lenin once stood,
I hear chatter and trade in Ukrainian

and Russian. Grubby gryvnya
and kopeks are exchanged
for cabbages, potatoes, bread

and pirated cassettes by Madonna,
Metallica and U2. Scarred
Gypsy children beg for food.

Above the crowd, I look at the ruins
of an ancient castle atop the mountain:
a Transylvanian fortress constructed

to repel Turkic invaders
over eight hundred years before
the communists came to power.

I understand little, just the mist clinging
to the Transcarpathians, birds singing,
the daily struggle for food and shelter.

These things are constant. I am like the wind.

Ayr

The bus from Glasgow to Stranraer
terminated unexpectedly in Ayr,
stranding us amidst beauty.

All the rooms in town were full.
After a dinner of fish and chips
we bought a dozen cans of Tennent's

and found a secluded site
on the beach, drank
hours of northern twilight.

When the moon was high
we unfurled sleeping bags,
pushed passports, pounds and pence

down to safety with our feet,
employed our backpacks as pillows
and went to sleep hoping

to remain unmolested.
Workers noisily collecting rubbish
woke us as the sun rose

illuminating the sublime
Firth of Clyde and Isle of Arran.

Blank Faces

Our first date
was supposed
to be a visit
to an exhibition
of portraits
by Cartier-Bresson.

I waited
at the underground
station for an hour,
but she didn't show.

Icy winds blasted
through the tunnels.
Trains not carrying her
rumbled below.
All the faces
in the crowd
were blank.

Slaving

Sitting outside
the kitchen
of a London pub,
peeling potatoes
in the October
afternoon sun,
I feel like Orwell.

Islington Dawn

On the cold floor of a borrowed flat
in Islington, we fumbled under
a well-travelled army surplus blanket.
Two Antipodeans drawn together
by a common culture in the foreign
capital of a decomposed empire,
we sought comfort and pleasure
amidst omnipresent grey.
Her ballerina's body graceless
while prone; my pale frame,
scarred by rugby and sun,
awkward and furtive with desire.
Hours after dawn, we sat together
in the courtyard on a bench covered
with graffiti, vainly searching
for escape in the morning drizzle.

Pozières

The Somme, early September, pouring rain.
Twenty-three thousand of my countrymen
were killed here over forty-one days,
fighting over paddocks
between this ridge
and that windmill.

I'm here paying homage
to my great-grandfather George
and his ANZAC mates who suffered here,
travelling from memorial to memorial,
from cemetery to swollen cemetery,
horrified by the stupidity
of the whole bloody thing.

George survived, made it home
to raise Merinos in Victoria,
but the mustard gas wrecked his lungs
and he died young, unable to escape
the consequences of other men's mistakes.

North Rhine-Westphalia

Long evenings around
the kitchen table fuelled
by Warsteiner, Becks
and Liebfraumilch
led to sharing a single bed
in a freezing barely furnished
farmhouse, pre-dawn walks
through cornfields into town,
countless journeys on the D-bahn,
S-bahn, U-bahn and Autobahn
to teaching gigs, and finally
to an Ikea-furnished apartment
on Goethestrasse
overlooking an art gallery,
Trinkhalle and a strip club.

Croagh Patrick

After hiking from Westport
to the base of the mountain
and stopping to lunch on Guinness
and shepherd's pie, it seemed foolish
to have come so far and not make
the climb. You wanted to rest
and sat by the coffin ship
monument. Not wanting to keep
you waiting too long, I ran
most of the way up, passing
crawling barefoot pilgrims
ascending on a different plane.
Near the top I met our Argentinean
roommate and we posed for photos
at the summit, the Atlantic glistening
behind us. Running back down,
I met you coming up, having decided
to climb after all. I turned, heading
up for the second unplanned ascent.
We circled the chapel then meditated
at the peak for half an hour, absorbing
the view before descending
and hiking back into Westport
as the sky turned to dusk
and Croagh Patrick disappeared
into the darkness behind us.

The Hill of Tara

Lacking a rag, I tied
a fresh white handkerchief
to a rag tree on the Hill of Tara,
thought a prayer
for my daughter,
taking comfort in a ritual
foreign to me, but routine
for my people, seeking
to connect through a simple
gesture to our ancestors
who ruled the land stretching
before me to the horizon.

Invisible Borders

for Sean

During the last week of December
we drove north from Dublin
between stone walls and hedges
bound for Bailieborough,
down through Greaghnadarragh
listening to the Irish language
radio station, not understanding
a word but loving the sounds.
Soft rain glistened on stones,
dripped from branches,
threatened to turn to ice.
On the main street of the village
my ancestors called home,
half the shops had my surname
written above the door
and half the pubs were closed.
We ate in the Bailie Hotel,
served fish, peas, potatoes
and pints by a distant relation.

Late in the afternoon, long past
Kingscourt, Carrickmacross,
and Patrick Kavanagh country,
you sat in the passenger seat
crossing the invisible border,
cradling a bottle of Aussie red
picked up at a petrol station
outside Dundalk. We drove
through the shadows
of the mountains of Mourne
down to Warrenpoint, searching
for your grandfather's summer
home in the gloaming as darkness
descended on Carlingford Lough.

We drove north, deeper
into the dark, through
Newtownhamilton, Lisnadill
and Armagh to Loughall,
where an old friend waited
with whiskey to guide us safely
across borders we could not see,
navigating cartography
visible only to a local.

St John's Wood

Every morning I paid
for breakfast at Café Rouge
with tips earned pulling pints
for the wealthy the night before.
I kept calm while they blabbered
about the glories of the Empire
and called me a *colonial*.

I shared a room with a Canadian
and two racist South Africans
next to a roomful of farm-raised Kiwis.
We drank together after closing time,
united in our whingeing about the Poms.

I blew fifty quid on gin and tonics
for two delectable Nova Scotians
just arrived from a gig in Galway,
despite not having Buckley's.

I shared newspapers in the library
with elderly gentlemen in bespoke suits
who read the *Financial Times*
and muttered about selling another Jag.

On my days off, I walked
through Primrose Hill to Camden Town
where I bought a CCCP T-shirt,
Docs, used Levis and Australian
novels, saw Nick Cave
getting pounds from an ATM,
got hammered in The World's End.

I bought international phone cards
from surly Pakistani newsagents,
made homesick midnight calls
to family, mates and old flames
in Melbourne, Sydney and Canberra.

I slept in other people's beds or dossed
in share-houses in Willesden Green,
Islington, Watford and Bayswater,
sometimes with an ex-ballerina
from Altona, but usually alone.

On the day I moved out,
I walked to the tube station
through floating snow,
on my way to Gatwick
and a plane waiting
to take me home to summer.

Skimming

for Joe

Stopping by the shallow stream
we bent to pick up stones,
tested their flatness in our hands,

felt their weight and size.
We selected the best,
took our places on the bank.

Arms drew back, knees bent,
a sudden flick of the wrists
sent our first volley flying.

After striking the clear cold water
the stones curved into the air,
dropped to hit the water again

and again and again, before
sinking to the bottom sighing.

York

I

Under the willow's boughs
we found shelter for the night.
Curtained behind drooping leaves
we fell asleep listening to rain.

After dawn, we awoke, stretched,
cast aside the wet branches.
The glassy river flowed
past our sanctuary, glistening.

II

We walked upon the ancient wall
which protected emperors and kings.
We felt its age with our palms:
images of battle bled through stone.

We breathed in history thick as fog,
saw visions of blood and elation.
Like the Romans, Vikings and Normans,
we came, we wondered, we disappeared.

Yorkshire Lunch

Crashing down through
the Land Rover's gears,
driving narrow roads
between stone walls
from Giggleswick
to Wigglesworth,
thoughts turn
to The Plough
and the pint of bitter
I will savour there.

I shall bask in the sun
at a picnic table
outside the front door.
I will sip my pint,
wipe froth from my lips
with the back of my hand,
gaze down the road
at the grazing sheep.

When I can no longer
deny the hunger earnt
during my morning ramble,
I shall order Yorkshire lamb
and sticky toffee pudding.
Satisfied, I will take my time
and savour straight whisky
before driving slowly home.

Côte d'Azur

for Tricia

During our last childless summer
we lay on the beach at Eze,
marvelling at the Mediterranean,
blue in the shadows of mansions.

On the stony beach
we glistened
in the late-morning sun,
salt crusting on skin.

Women speaking French,
Italian and German lounged
and strolled the beach topless,
nonchalant in near-nudity.

Men in tiny, shameless speedos
rubbed oil into their bellies,
shoulders, legs and arms, sprawled
at ease, sipping Stella Artois.

We swam out past the buoys
and floated on our backs facing
the shore, scanning the hillside
for the home of our dreams.

America

At the Hair Salon in Big Sandy, Texas

A warm stomach rests
on my arm. Breasts squish
against my shoulder blades.
Fingers fold ears, gently
but firmly lift my chin.
The clippers' power cord
tightens against my neck,
stretching to the outlet.
Without glasses,
I'm a blond and black blur
in the mirror.
Spraying a fine mist,
the hairdresser grips
scissors, drawls –
*You ain't from around here,
is ya? Where y'all from?*
        – Australia
Neat! Did y'all drive?
        – No, it's a bit far. I had to fly.
*You speak English real good.
Did y'all learn it in school?*

Blue

After midnight by the lakeside
we argued about that shirt,
my floral favourite I bought
last summer in Temple Bar.

I thought it was hip
in a retro kind of way,
but you said it wasn't manly,
even with blue flowers.

I yelled in defence of my shirt,
but of course the argument
had nothing to do with flowers,
fashion, nostalgia and colours.

The conflict went deeper,
all the way down to childhood,
religion, family politics, gender
norms, culture and nationality.

Disintegration

We fell apart in Los Angeles,
disintegrated between Christmas
and New Year's Eve.

Years of life shared in Europe
and America were not enough
to hold us together.

We argued about spending
habits, financial responsibility,
nationalism, career choices.

You pleaded for me to change,
wept in the rain on Colorado Avenue,
oblivious to revellers' stares.

I felt despair descending,
smothering me as you sobbed,
shook, shivered on the sidewalk.

The Woods

We entered armed
with wine, a knife,
cheese, crackers, cigars,
a lighter, your photographs
and my poetry. You dressed
in black, down to the boots.

We gathered wood,
built the fire as one.
Warmed by orange flames,
mellowed by cheese and wine,
we reclined and conversed
until darkness descended.

House Sitting

A wooden, two-storey house with three bedrooms,
kitchen, dining room, living room, two bathrooms,
study, lake-view balcony, polished floors,
cathedral ceilings, Venetian blinds,
ceiling fans and a grill on the back deck.

A smiling woman at an outdoor café
in Alexanderplatz. A golden retriever
in a red convertible. A balding man
in a black suit standing before a tree.
An elderly woman at a university graduation.

Prints by O'Keefe, Chagall and Kandinsky.
A model sailboat. Wooden giraffes.
Greek currency. A Gorbachev Russian doll.
Unopened mail from Harvard University.
An Apple computer. Bose speakers.

Deutsch–English and Français–Anglais
dictionaries. Indian, Thai and Greek
cookbooks. Organic sauces
and herbal teas. Dozens of jars
of spices and bottles of vitamins.

Ikea, Pier 1 and House of Denmark
furniture. Leather couches and armchairs,
tubular steel and glass tables,
wooden bookshelves. Forty-four
cents between the couch cushions.

Sheet music. A piano and three guitars.
B.B. King. Beethoven. Thelonius Monk.
Mozart. Dianna Krall. Eminem.
Dave Brubeck. Stevie Ray Vaughan.
Chuck Berry. The Beatles. Cream.

The Art of War. The Fall of Yugoslavia.
The Tin Drum. The Intelligence Enigma.
Europe. Moscow. Greece. Berlin.
Casino Royale. Small World.
Into Thin Air. Fast Food Nation.

Real Simple. Cosmopolitan.
Scientific American.
American Scientist.
Newsweek. Cooking Light.
Bon Appetit.

Dr Strangelove.
The Constant Gardener.
The Matrix. Dr No.
Donnie Darko.
Star Wars.

Bombay Sapphire. Jose Cuervo.
Jim Beam. Absolut.
Oberon. Guinness.
Blue Moon. Moosehead.
Leinenkugel's.

Two Swiss army knives.
A map of ski runs in the Swiss Alps.
Cross-country skis, boots and poles.
A mountain bike, a wetsuit and a kayak.
A yoga mat and an open Durex box.

Texas Life

We loaded the car in L.A.
and set off for Texas.
It seemed far enough away
from anywhere of importance.
Out there we could create
a private universe
among the lakes and pines.
We bought a trailer
on a secluded acre,
disappeared for a year.

It was the perfect way to start
a marriage: a secret life
without distractions.
We didn't need more excitement;
there was enough between us.
Our books, music, beer
and bodies kept us happy.

Michigan

for Tricia

We traded Texas heat for Michigan snow;
finally, one of us was home. One morning
you woke me, calling to say you'd hit a deer
on your way to work. I rushed into clothes
and sped through cornfields to hold you.

We spent our second anniversary in Saugatuck,
luxuriated in bathrobes, ate crackers in bed,
shared the Jacuzzi, climbed the lookout, walked Oval Beach,
strolled the boardwalk, lusted after yachts from Chicago.

We drove north to camp, climbed Sleeping Bear Dunes,
lay on a half-deflated air mattress listening for bobcats.
We drove by shimmering lakes, vineyards, red barns
and clichéd postcard-perfect towns, stopping at casinos
where you pushed coins into slots while strangers
bought me drinks because they liked my accent.
We crossed the Mackinac Bridge, drove north across
the Upper Peninsula to Sault Ste Marie, watched
a Norwegian ship pass through the locks.

We took trips to Canada, Mexico, Ireland, Australia
and France, where you lay topless on the beach
as vendors shouted *Coca-Cola, Fanta, Orangeeeena!*
We spent days on our backs in the salty turquoise
Mediterranean, savoured the local wine and cuisine,
strolled along cobbled streets while I fantasised
about owning an apartment with shutters on the windows,
spending every summer on the Cote d'Azur.

After two years in Michigan we bought our first house,
spent hundreds of hours and thousands of dollars
renovating every room together. We ambled hand in hand
along the river walk, through streets lined with historic homes,
ate ice cream at the fountain. We soaked in our hot tub,
drank martinis and margaritas as snow settled around us.

Reminders

Framed black and white photographs
of trams rattling downhill
through fog on suburban streets
and stopping beside palm trees

hang on the wall beside Luna Park,
Ballarat, Tower Hill, Port Fairy,
Mount Macedon and the Grampians –

reminders of a life left behind,
connections to places no longer
part of everyday life, ancestors

decomposed in graveyards,
friendships suffering entropy,
halcyon days impossible to recover.

Cupcakes and Monsters

for Celeste

Drawing on the back
of a copy of the Jerilderie Letter,
you craft cupcakes and monsters,
unaware of the document's significance,
of language's ability to span
centuries and continents.

Grasping crayons, you are unaware
of your dual nationality,
your roots in Ireland, Wales, England,
Australia and the Netherlands.
For now, your world is light
as a cupcake, harmless
as a sketched monster.

Free

Alone at last
with silence
space and time

Free from demands
responsibilities
and deadlines

Free to think and create
open to new perceptions
and influences

Free to sit and stare
at mountains and mesas
through crisp azure air

Rosemary and Gasoline

As my drunk friend
pours fuel onto the barbecue,
the flame leaps up
into the can and he turns
flinging gasoline
across the backyard
towards the hedge of rosemary.

Beer in hand, I dash
across the lawn, stomping
out flames with boots.
Turning as I run, I slip
on gasoline, land on my back,
slide towards the fence.

Friends yell *You're on fire!*
as I regain my feet.
I dive-roll, tumbling,
coming to rest as friends'
wives aim the garden hose
towards me and turn the faucet.

Somehow unscathed, I stand,
gratefully accept another beer.
The aroma of rosemary and gasoline
scents the suburban summer air
as I listen to eyewitness accounts
of my shirt aflame, wishing
someone had captured the moment.

Cancer in Suburbia

When the neighbourhood kids
wrapped my next-door neighbour's
Live Oak in toilet paper
late on Saturday night,
did they know she
was inside her house
fighting cancer?
Did they know she
has barely ventured outside
in months, that the affluent
exterior of her home masks
the tragedy of a newlywed
wrestling the angel of death?

Christian Girls

Christian girls with crosses
dangling in the depths
of exposed cleavage
sit silently in the front row,
hands crossed in laps,
eyes raised towards the speaker,
lips sealed in a half-smile.

As they lean forward
to hear the word,
their crosses swing out
into open space –
then back to rest
in the valley of the shadow
as bodies become upright.

West Texas

Cotton fields, meat processing plants,
oil derricks, barbed-wire fences,
power lines, oil and gas pipelines
clutter the landscape from Amarillo
to Lubbock, Sweetwater to Abilene.
Round here, resource extraction
trumps aesthetics.

Highways pass majestic mesas,
canyons, and ranches the size
of English counties. Longhorns
laze amidst cacti in the shadows
of wind turbines.

Beside a remote highway
heading south towards Mexico
a faded billboard from the nineties
declares *He don't inhale, he just sucks*
while extracted oil speeds past
on trains bound for gulf coast refineries.

Hybridity

Whiskey on ice.
Kavanagh. Heaney.
Ghalib's ghazals.
English, Gaelic,
Urdu and Norse
blend in the study
of a darkening house.

Reunions

Infrequent gatherings
with old friends
in Sydney, New York, Dublin,
Toronto and Houston
ease the pain of separation,
provide a temporary cure
for the expatriate condition.

The moments together
allow us to forget
the years and decades
spent as aliens amidst
strangers unable
to understand our lives.

Drinking pints in the snug
comfort of decades-long
friendship, we quickly forget
missing births, marriages,
birthdays, anniversaries,
Christmas, beachside family
reunions, deaths and funerals.

Expat Christmas

My wife is in the kitchen
singing 'How To Make Gravy'
while I drink Jacob's Creek
and eat salt and vinegar chips,
ten thousand miles from home

the day after my youngest sister
gave birth to Evie, my first niece –
another family member
I will only know from afar –
for whom I will play the role

of distant relative, absent uncle,
making holiday appearances
every three years on average,
sending presents in the mail,
commenting on status updates.

I will stay with my American
family in my American house
going to my American job,
listening to Paul Kelly,
eating Vegemite, drinking
Penfolds and Coopers,
attempting to destroy the distance
between my past and my present.

Nathanael O'Reilly was born in Warrnambool and raised in Ballarat, Brisbane and Shepparton. He now resides in Texas. His previous publications include two chapbooks, *Suburban Exile: American Poems* (2011) and *Symptoms of Homesickness* (2010), both published by Picaro Press, and over one hundred poems in journals and anthologies around the world. He is the recipient of an Emerging Writers Grant from the Literature Board of the Australia Council for the Arts.

www.ingramcontent.com/pod-product-compliance
Lightning Source LLC
Chambersburg PA
CBHW062140100526
44589CB00014B/1639